FREE GOODIES!

EMAIL US AT

sightwords@scholdeners.com

**And we'll send you extra worksheets plus
a list of hundreds of additional sight words**

200

WRITE-AND-LEARN

SIGHT WORDS

Contents

Introduction

List of 200 Sight Words

I	we	let	who	have	open	will	these
a	all	man	why	here	over	wish	thing
am	and	may	you	high	play	with	think
an	any	men	also	home	read	work	three
as	are	new	away	into	said	year	under
at	big	not	back	just	seem	your	until
be	box	old	ball	kind	some	about	where
by	boy	one	been	know	soon	after	which
do	but	our	best	left	such	again	while
go	can	out	book	like	sure	black	white
he	day	own	both	live	take	bring	would
if	did	put	call	last	tell	color	before
in	ear	ran	came	long	than	could	better
is	eat	red	come	look	that	first	friend
it	end	run	dear	made	them	found	little
me	far	saw	down	make	then	house	mother
my	for	say	each	many	they	leave	people
no	get	see	find	more	this	never	please
of	got	she	five	most	tree	night	pretty
on	had	the	four	much	upon	other	school
or	has	too	from	must	very	right	should
so	her	two	girl	name	want	shall	another
to	him	use	give	near	were	stand	because
up	his	was	good	next	what	their	morning
us	how	way	hand	only	when	there	present

Introduction

What are sight words?

Sight words in early learning refer to a set of words that constantly appear on almost any page of writing. You could call them the building blocks of written language. A few examples of sight words are 'who, he, the, were, does, their, me, be'.

In addition to being found very frequently in written text, many sight words cannot be 'sounded out'. Words such as 'come, does' and 'who' do not follow the standard rules of spelling. The simplest and most effective way to learn the words is by memory. Children are encouraged to memorize sight words as a whole, by sight, so that they recognize them immediately without having to decode the spelling.

The problem is that this means minimal instruction is given by teachers and parents. Often little more is done than showing the word to the child and telling them what it is. However for many children, this is not nearly enough. As a result, their reading and comprehension of these crucial words is lacking, which brings down their overall reading ability.

The best way to learn

The key to mastering these essential words is spending time with your child to ensure that they gain a deep understanding of them. The best technique for achieving this is accurate writing and spelling of the sight word, understanding its use in a simple sentence, and a visual representation of the phrase to reinforce how the word is used in context. This forms a multi-dimensional model for the child to really grasp the sight word, along with its spelling, meaning and usage.

In teaching terms, giving your child the opportunity to learn words in context is known as 'meaningful reading'. This is an extremely effective tool that has been shown to be far superior to plain memorization or rote learning.

DOLCH SIGHT WORDS LIST ✔

Educator Dr Edward William Dolch developed the 'Dolch Sight Words List' by studying the most frequently occurring words in children's books. These words comprise a staggering 80% of the words you would find in a standard children's book. Once a child knows this list of words, it makes reading much easier. You'll be pleased to know that this book incorporates the key Dolch words.

Using this book

Layout of pages

The sight word

A simple sentence using the sight word

Trace the word in top line

Now practise writing the word over two lines

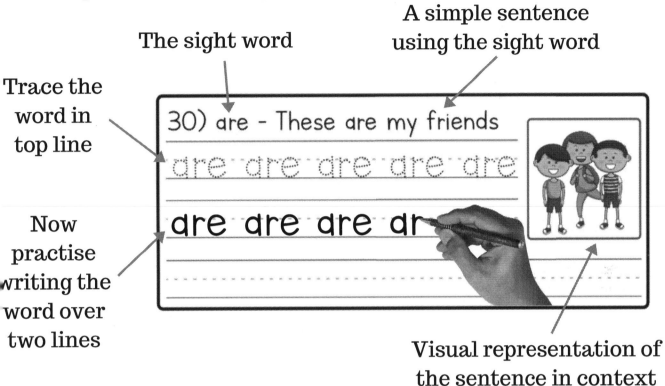

Visual representation of the sentence in context

This workbook takes a multi-pronged strategy to teaching sight words. For each word, we see it used in a simple sentence for context, and there's also an illustration to reinforce this understanding. The child then traces the dotted words on the top line before practising writing them free-hand in the remaining two lines. We encourage parents to review the work and discuss the sight words and illustrations with the child to reinforce learning.

Mastering letters

Before diving into the sight words, let's take the time to practise our letters. After all, letters are the basic building blocks of words. Once we have mastered each letter – both uppercase and lower case – writing words will be much easier!

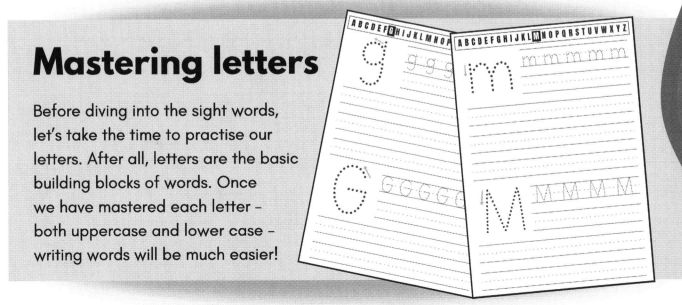

Part 1: Practice letters

Before we tackle the sight words, let's quickly go over each of our letters.

Trace the dotted letters on the top line, then write them in the remaining space.

The arrow shows you where to start.

a a a a a a a

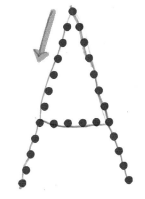

A A A A A A

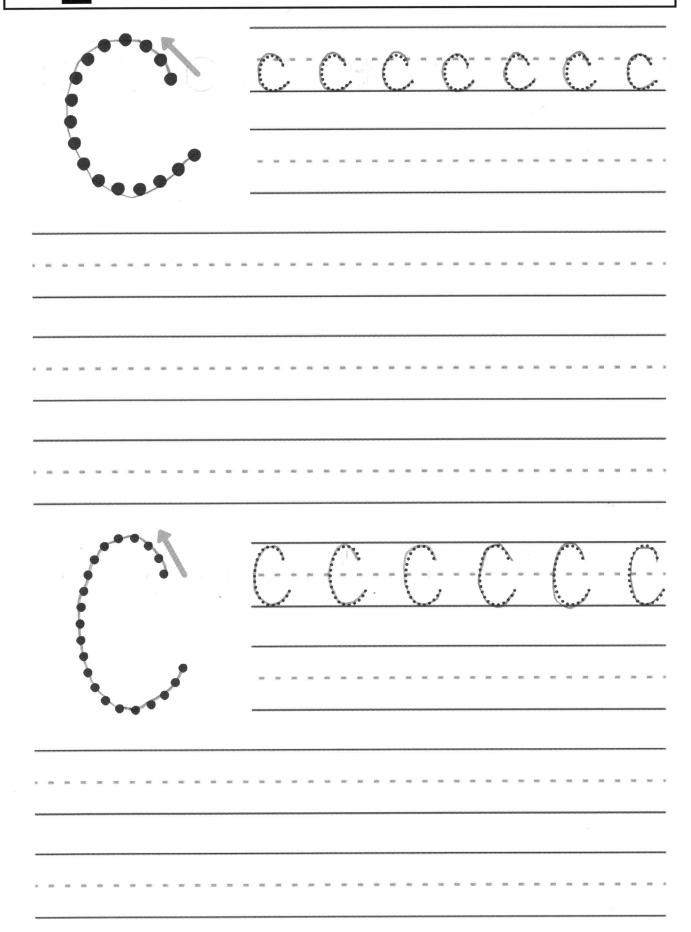

A B C D **E** F G H I J K L M N O P Q R S T U V W X Y Z

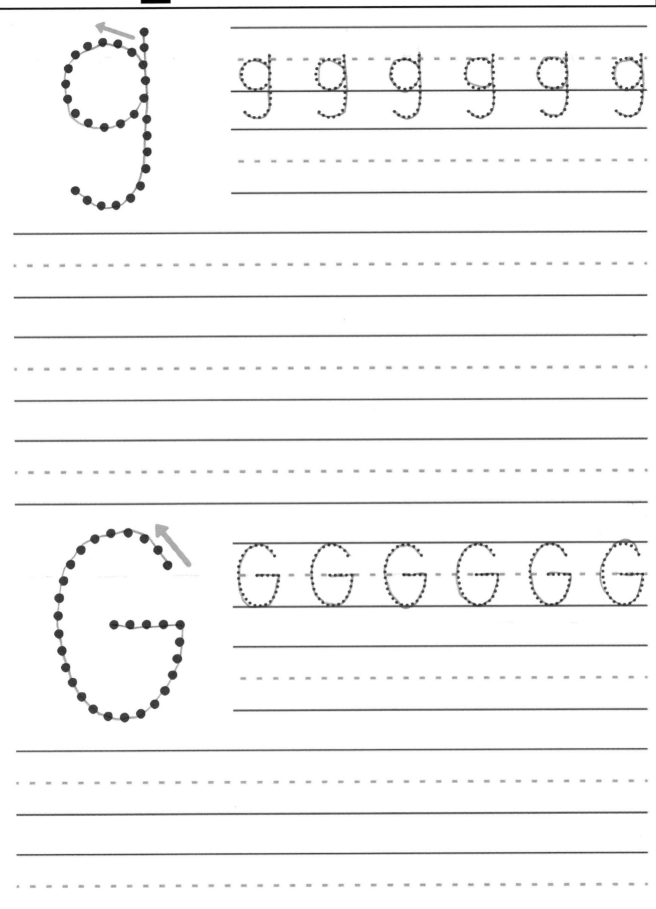

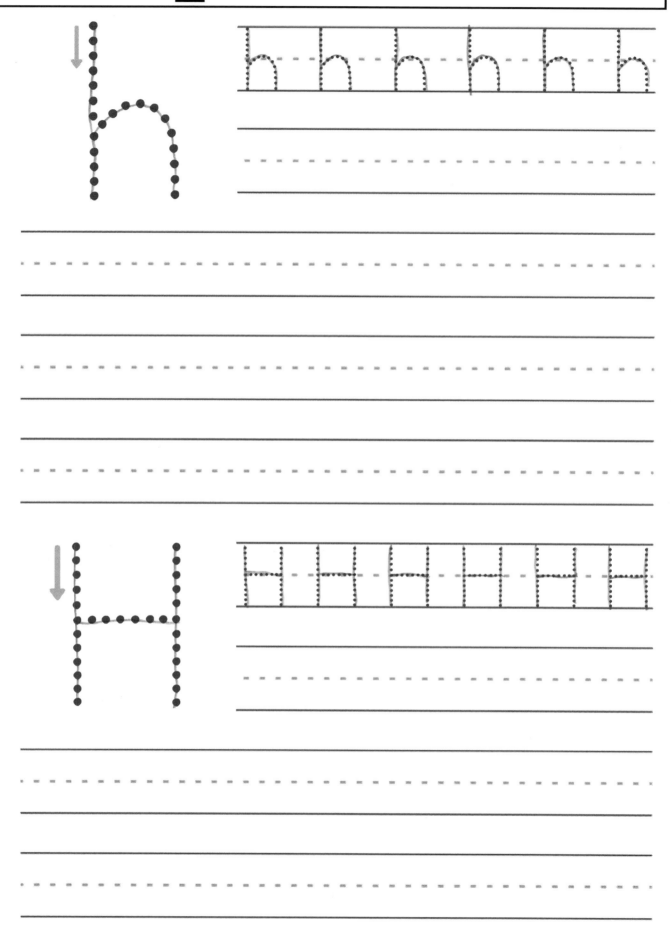

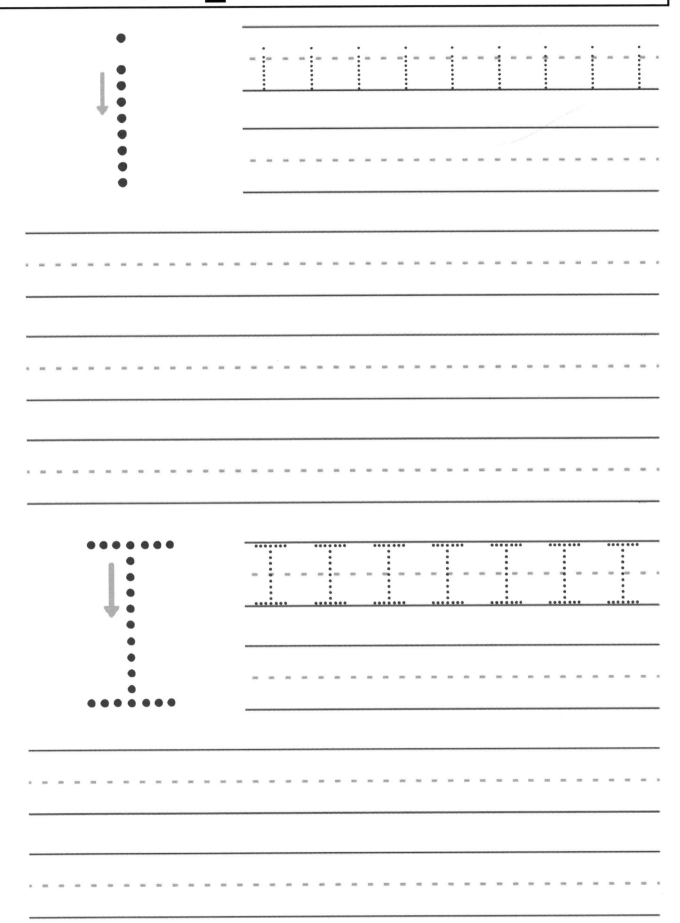

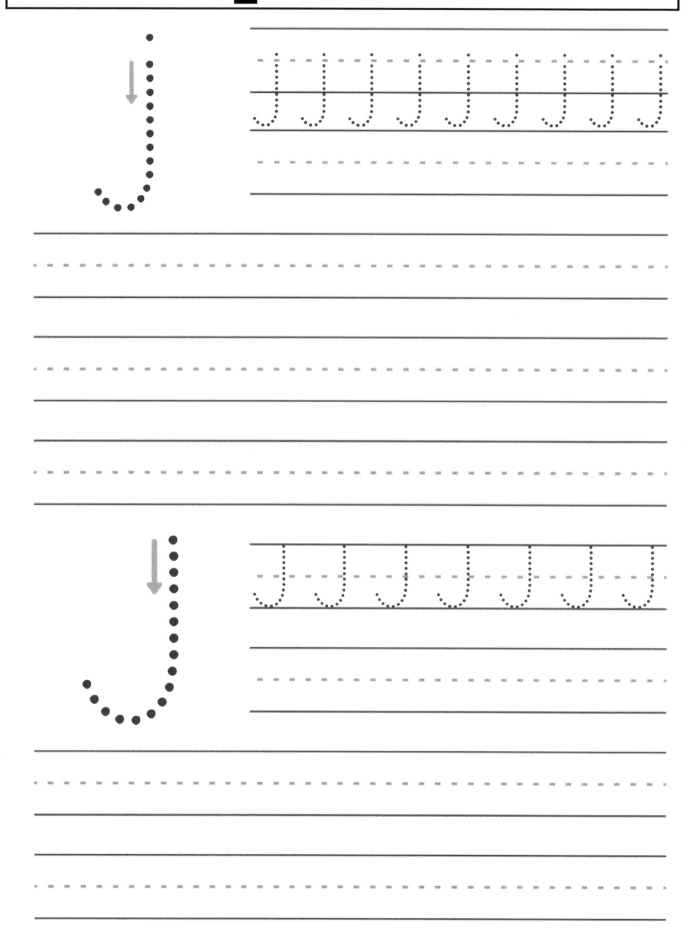

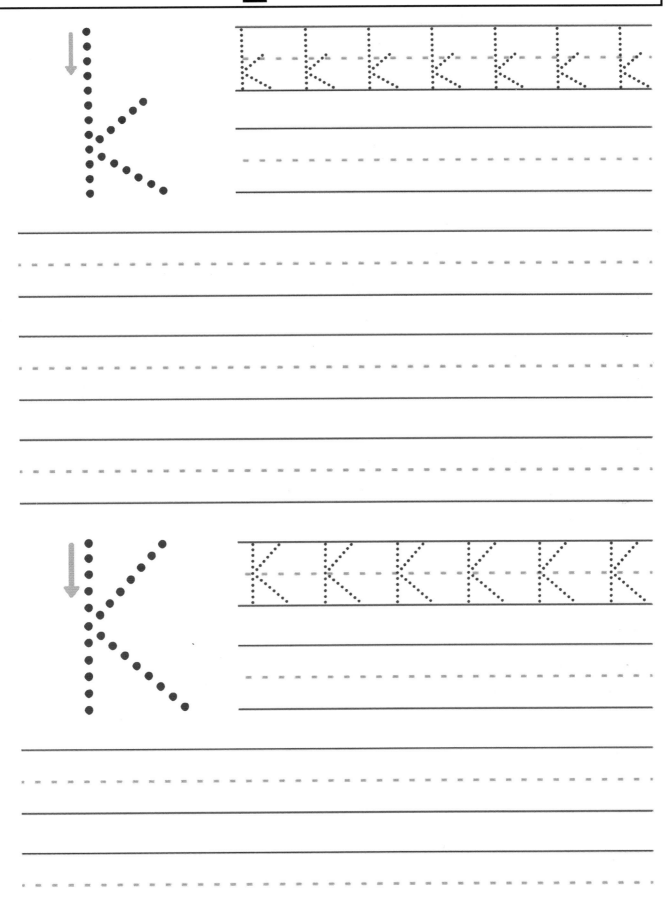

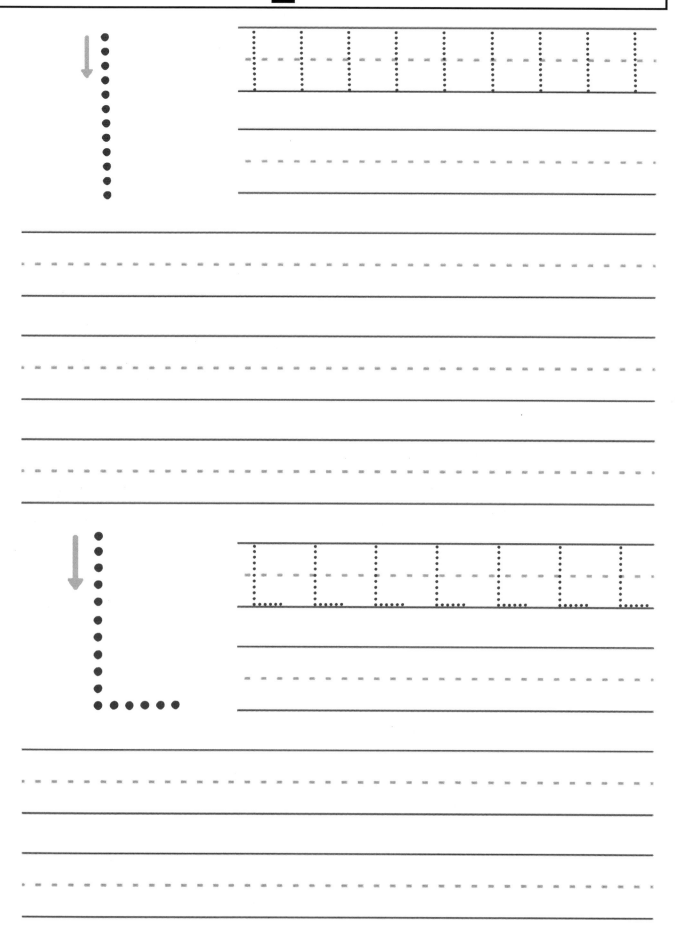

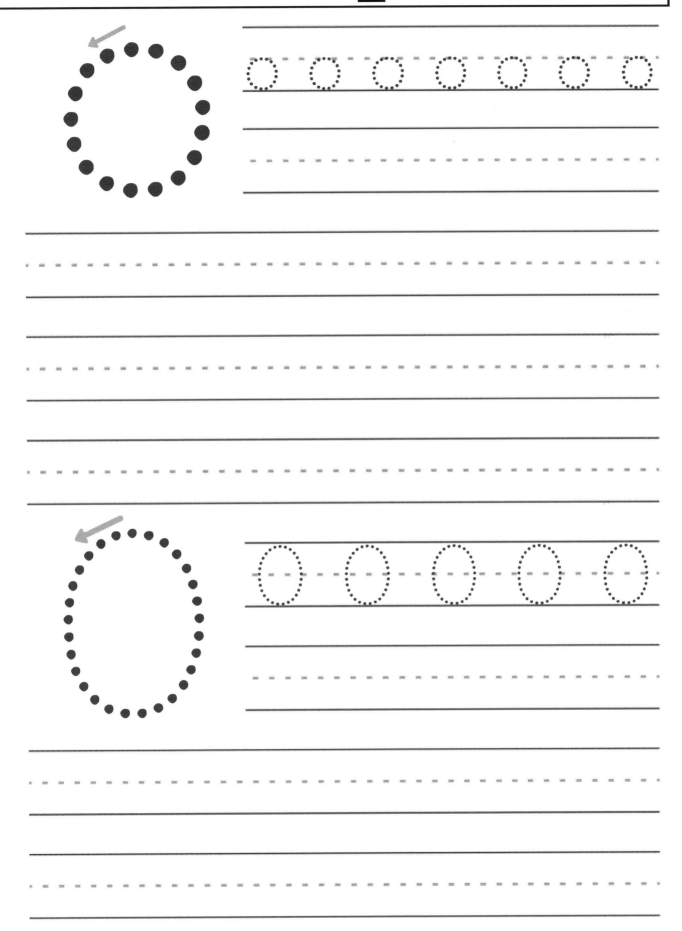

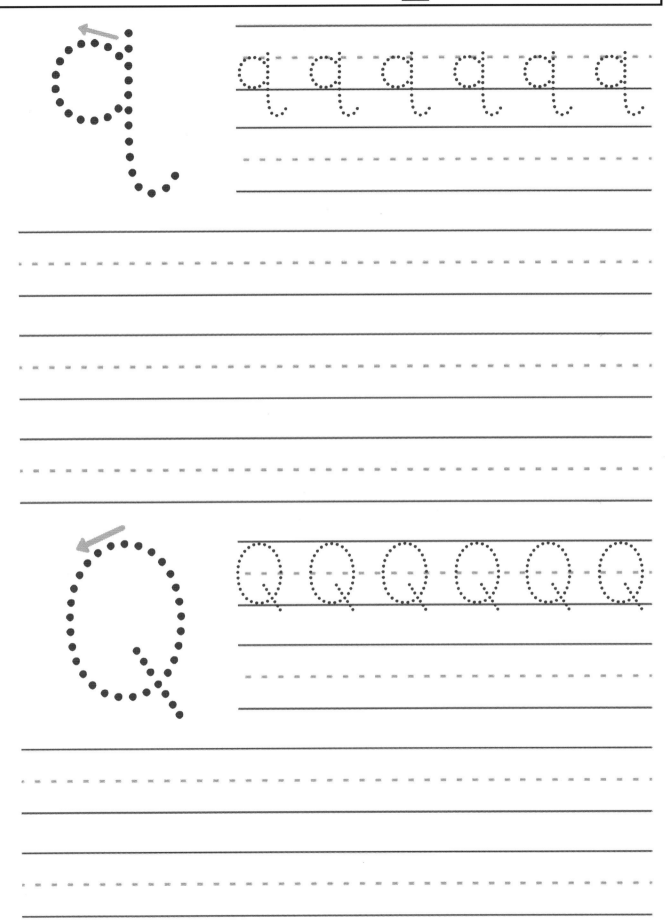

A B C D E F G H I J K L M N O P Q R S T U V W X Y Z

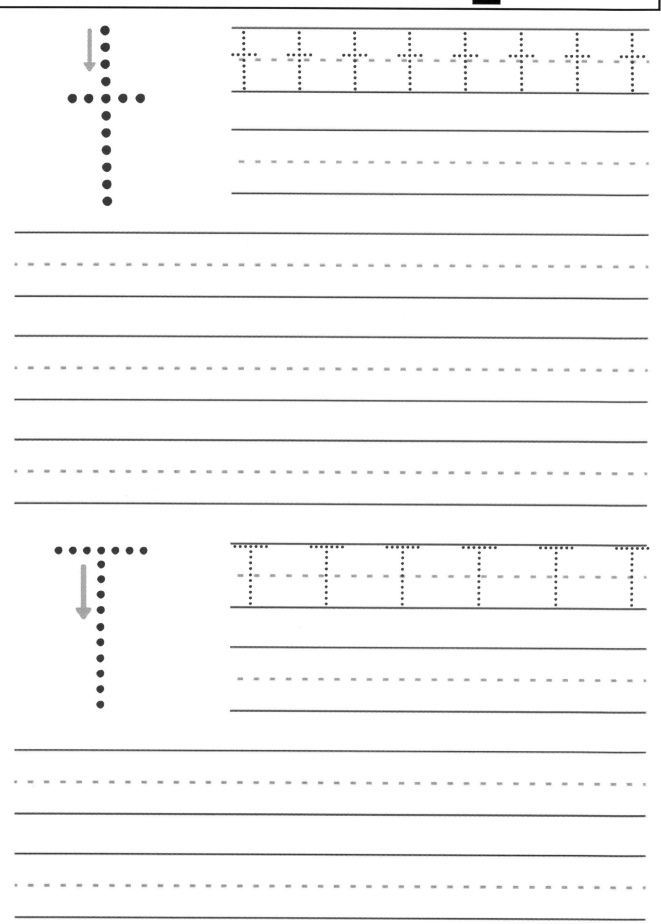

A B C D E F G H I J K L M N O P Q R S T U V W X Y Z

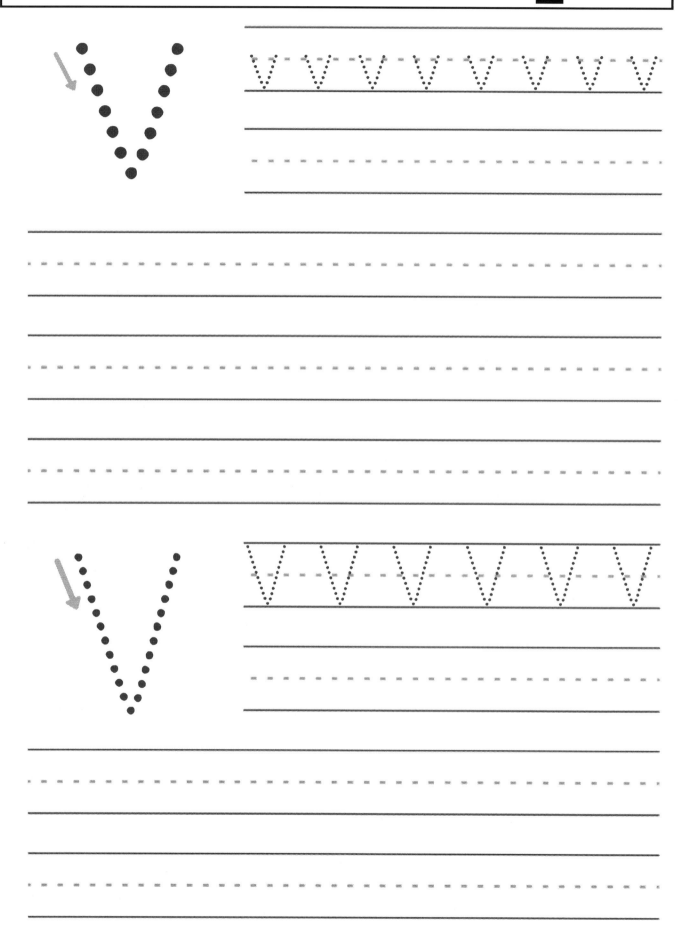

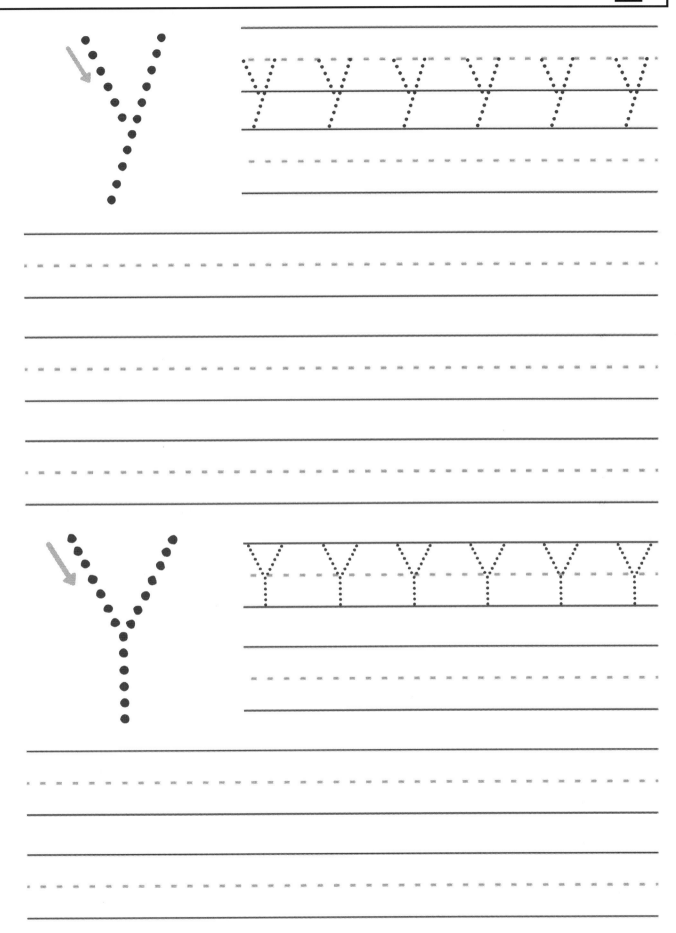

Part 2: Sight Words

Look at the sight word and then read the sentence to see how it is used (ask for help if you need it).

Now trace the dotted word on the top line and then write it yourself in the remaining space.

1) a – This is a great book

a a a a a a a a a a a

2) I – I have got the flu

I I I I I I I I I I I

3) am – I am very clever

am am am am am

4) an - I drew an angel

an an an an an an

5) as - I'm happy as can be

as as as as as as as

6) at - Meet me at the cinema

at at at at at at at

7) be - I will be a doctor

be be be be be be

8) by - This drawing is by me

by by by by by by

9) do - Let's do nothing today

do do do do do do

10) go - Time to go to school

go go go go go go

11) he - Can he jump higher?

he he he he he he

12) if - Let's see if she can dance

if if if if if if if if if

13) in - It's cozy in my bed

in in in in in in in in

14) is - This is my mother

is is is is is is is is

15) it - I hope it is sunny today

it it it it it it it it

16) me - I like being me!

me me me me me

17) my - Meet my lovely dog

my my my my my

18) no - Say no to bullying

no no no no no no

19) of - I'm a fan of hockey

of of of of of of of

20) on - I'm on top of the world

on on on on on on

21) or - I want fries or rice

or or or or or or or

22) so - She is so happy today

so so so so so so so

23) to - Let's go to the library

to to to to to to to

24) up - The rocket shot up

up up up up up up

25) us - Join us in the park

us us us us us us us

26) we - Today we visit grandma

we we we we we we

27) all - This is all my money

all all all all all all all

28) and - This is mom and dad

and and and and and

29) any - I like any kind of music

any any any any any

30) are - These are my friends

are are are are are

31) big - That's a big smile!

big big big big big

32) box - What's inside the box?

box box box box box

33) boy - My new sibling is a boy

boy boy boy boy boy

34) but - Ride, but be careful

but but but but but

35) can - I can do a cartwheel

can can can can can

36) day - Will it be a rainy day?

day day day day day

37) did - I did all my homework

did did did did did

38) ear - I like to wear ear muffs

ear ear ear ear ear

39) eat - What will we eat tonight?

eat eat eat eat eat

40) end - I saw the race end

end end end end

41) far - How far can you see?

far far far far far

42) for - Is that gift for me?

for for for for for

43) get – I hope you get better

get get get get get

44) got – The robber got caught

got got got got got

45) had – He had the best grades

had had had had

46) has - Dad has a bass guitar

has has has has has

47) her - This is her magic trick

her her her her her

48) him - Tell him to be quiet

him him him him

49) his – This is his pet bunny

his his his his his

50) how – I like how he plays

how how how how

51) let – Dad let me use his bike

let let let let let

52) man - The man wears glasses

man man man man

53) may - I may go swimming

may may may may

54) men - The men dressed well

men men men men

55) new - I love my new phone

new new new new

56) not - I am not very well today

not not not not not

57) old - Dad's computer is so old

old old old old old

58) one - I only have one brother

one one one one

59) our - This is our new house

our our our our our

60) out - She took out her phone

out out out out out

61) own - I have my own room

own own own own

62) put - Please put down the box

put put put put put

63) ran - Mom ran to the shops

ran ran ran ran ran

64) red - Apples are often red

red red red red red

65) run - He can run really fast

run run run run run

66) saw - I saw my grandpa today

saw saw saw saw

67) say - I had to say goodbye

say say say say say

68) see - I can see much better

see see see see see

69) she - Is she a good teacher?

she she she she she

70) the - I love the theatre

the the the the the

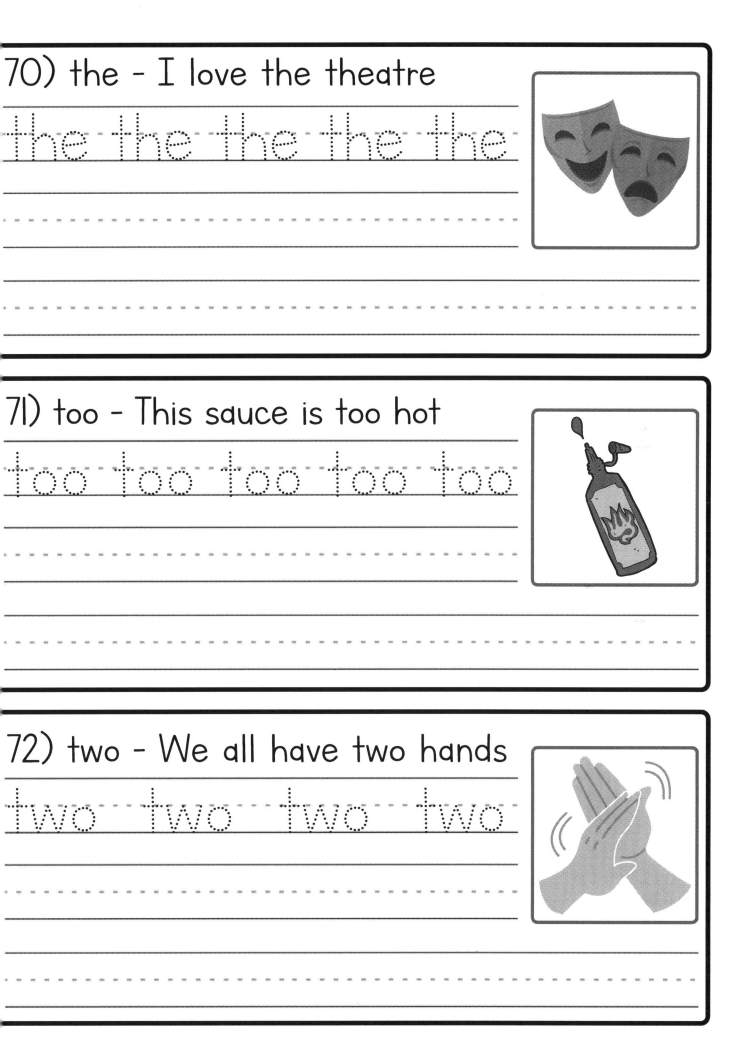

71) too - This sauce is too hot

too too too too too

72) two - We all have two hands

two two two two

73) use - I use a calculator often

use use use use use

74) was - This was where we lived

was was was was

75) way - Is this the way home?

way way way way

76) who - This is who I am

who who who who

77) why - I know why it rains

why why why why

78) you - Do you like to sing?

you you you you

79) also - I'm also a superhero!

also also also also

80) away - Let's get away today

away away away

81) back - Come back soon

back back back

82) ball - Keep control of the ball

ball ball ball ball

83) been - I've been very good

been been been

84) best - This is my best scarf

best best best best

85) book - I read a book with dad

book book book

86) both - I love both my sisters

both both both

87) call - Can I call you tonight?

call call call call call

88) came - He came to my house

came came came

89) come - Try to come tonight

come come come

90) dear - She is so dear to us

dear dear dear dear

91) down - The snow falls down

down down down

92) each - We have an apple each

each each each

93) find - Can you find my house?

find find find find

94) five - I have five pencils

five five five five

95) four - Hold up four fingers

four four four four

96) from - This is from me to you

from from from

97) girl - The girl loves to read

girl girl girl girl girl

98) give - Can you give me a hand?

give give give give

99) good - Your writing is very good

good good good

100) hand – This is my hand print

hand hand hand

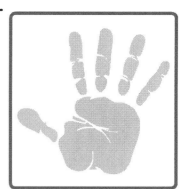

101) have – I have lots of homework

have have have have

102) here – Wish you were here

here here here here

103) high - She can jump so high

high high high high

104) home - I'm staying at home

home home home

105) into - Let's walk into the shop

into into into into

106) just - I just had my dinner

just just just just

107) kind - Let's be kind in life

kind kind kind kind

108) know - I know karate

know know know

109) left - I left my book at school

left left left left

110) like - I like to eat sushi

like like like like like

111) live - I live in a nice town

live live live live live

112) last - I went dancing last night

last last last last

113) long - There's a long way to go

long long long long

114) look - I look cool in a costume

look look look look

115) made - I made finger puppets

made made made

116) make - Help me make a cake

make make make

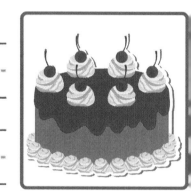

117) many - I have many friends

many many many

118) more - Can I have more fries?

more   more   more

119) most - I like her the most

most   most   most

120) much - That's too much food

much much much

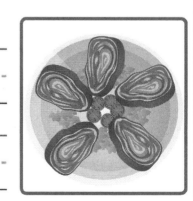

121) must - I must do my work

must must must

122) name - What's your name?

name name name

123) near - I live near a church

near near near near

124) next - What show is on next?

next next next next

125) only - This is my only tie

only only only only

126) open - Do not open the door

open open open

KEEP OUT!

127) over - Is the scary part over?

over over over over

128) play - Do you play tennis?

play play play play

129) read - She read those books

read read read read

130) said - She said how she felt

said said said said

131) seem - You seem a little sad

seem seem seem

132) some - I'd like some soup

some some some

133) soon - My trip ended too soon

said said said said

134) such - She's such a nice girl

seem seem seem

135) sure - I'm sure I want salad

some some some

136) take - Can you take a picture?

take take take take

137) tell - Let me tell you a secret

tell tell tell tell tell

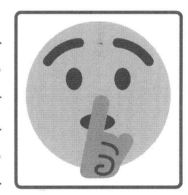

138) than - I'm taller than her

than than than than

139) that - I love that music

that that that that

140) them - See them looking cool

them them them

141) then - He smiled, then ran

then then then then

142) they – I think they dress well

they they they they

143) this – I like to sit like this

this this this this

144) tree – Look at that tall tree

tree tree tree tree

145) upon - You can rely upon mom

they they they they

146) very - I like her very much

this this this this

147) want - I want to be taller

tree tree tree tree

148) were - They were in a band

were were were

149) what - I like what I'm hearing

what what what

150) when - Call me when you can

when when when

151) will - He will go swimming

will will will will will

152) wish - I wish I could fly

wish wish wish wish

153) with - Me with my pet bunny

with with with with

154) work - Dad is going to work

work   work   work

155) year - I will be nine next year

year year year year

156) your - This is your Xmas gift

your your your your

157) about - He is about my age

about about about

158) after - We ran after the thief

after after after

159) again - It's raining again!

again again again

160) black - The cat is black

black black black

161) bring - Bring a kite to the park

bring bring bring

162) color - I like to color shapes

color color color

163) could - I wish I could swim

could could could

164) first - He got the first prize

first first first first

165) found - I found the test hard

found found found

166) house - That's a small house

house house house

167) leave - We must leave early

leave leave leave

168) never - You'll never be alone

never never never

169) night – A full moon at night

night　night　night

170) other – They know each other

other　other　other

171) right – I gave the right answer

right　right　right

172) shall - When shall we eat?

shall shall shall shall

173) stand - I can stand straight

stand stand stand

174) their - I met their new baby

their their their

175) there - He sits there often

there there there

176) these - Can you mail these?

these these these

177) thing - I can't see a thing

thing thing thing

178) think – I think you are right

think think think

179) three – I borrowed three books

three three three

180) under – Go under the umbrella

under under under

181) until - I slept until noon

until until until until

182) where - I wonder where he is?

where where where

183) which - So which tooth hurts?

which which which

184) while - Be quiet while I sleep

while while while

185) white - My pet bunny is white

white white white

186) would - I knew I would win

would would would

187) before - I read before dinner

before before before

188) better - I feel better today

better better better

189) friend - She's a good friend

friend friend friend

190) little - I have a little money

little little little little

191) mother - Meet my nice mother

mother   mother

192) people - A big crowd of people

people people people

193) please – Dad, help me please

please please please

194) pretty – That's a pretty dress

pretty pretty pretty

195) school – I love my new school

school school school

196) should - He should head home

should should should

197) another - Have another cookie

another   another

198) because - I do it because I can

because   because

199) morning - What a nice morning

morning morning

200) present - Be present at school

present present

201) bonus - this is my bonus word!

bonus bonus bonus

Part 3: Practice Paper

Use this blank practice paper to go over any of the sight words again.

You can also use it to write your own interesting sentences.

Made in the USA
San Bernardino,
CA